Chance of
LIGHTNING

PREVIOUS WINNERS OF THE VASSAR MILLER PRIZE IN POETRY

Scott Cairns, Founding Editor
John Poch, Series Editor

Partial Eclipse by Tony Sanders
Selected by Richard Howard

Delirium by Barbara Hamby
Selected by Cynthia Macdonald

The Sublime by Jonathan Holden
Selected by Yusef Komunyakaa

American Crawl by Paul Allen
Selected by Sydney Lea

Soul Data by Mark Svenvold
Selected by Heather McHugh

Moving & St Rage by Kathy Fagan
Selected by T. R. Hummer

A Protocol for Touch
   by Constance Merritt
Selected by Eleanor Wilner

The Perseids by Karen Holmberg
Selected by Sherod Santos

The Self as Constellation
   by Jeanine Hathaway
Selected by Madeline DeFrees

Bene-Dictions by Rush Rankin
Selected by Rosanna Warren

Losing and Finding by Karen Fiser
Selected by Lynne McMahon

The Black Beach by J. T. Barbarese
Selected by Andrew Hudgins

re-entry by Michael White
Selected by Paul Mariani

The Next Settlement
   by Michael Robins
Selected by Anne Winters

Mister Martini by Richard Carr
Selected by Naomi Shihab Nye

Ohio Violence by Alison Stine
Selected by Eric Pankey

Stray Home by Amy M. Clark
Selected by Beth Ann Fennelly

Circles Where the Head Should Be
   by Caki Wilkinson
Selected by J. D. McClatchy

Death of a Ventriloquist
   by Gibson Fay-LeBlanc
Selected by Lisa Russ Spaar

Club Icarus by Matt W. Miller
Selected by Major Jackson

In the Permanent Collection
   by Stefanie Wortman
Selected by Chad Davidson

Other Psalms by Jordan Windholz
Selected by Averill Curdy

Booker's Point by Megan Grumbling
Selected by Morri Creech

Ornament by Anna Lena Phillips Bell
Selected by Geoffrey Brock

The Goat Songs by James Najarian
Selected by A. E. Stallings

Dream Kitchen by Owen McLeod
Selected by Rosanna Warren

Instructions for Seeing a Ghost by
   Steve Bellin-Oka
Selected by Peter Balakian

Every Lash by Leigh Anne Couch
Selected by Jenny Browne

Door to Remain by Austin Segrest
Selected by Kark Kirchwey

Storm Swimmer by Ernest Hilbert
Selected by Rowan Ricardo Phillips

Felling by Kelan Nee
Selected by Gregory Fraser

Chance of
LIGHTNING

Kristin Robertson

Winner 2024 Vassar Miller Prize in Poetry

University of North Texas Press
Denton, Texas

Permissions:
University of North Texas Press
1155 Union Circle #311336
Denton, TX 76203-5017

The paper used in this book meets the minimum requirements of the American National Standard for Permanence of Paper for Printed Library Materials, z39.48.1984. Binding materials have been chosen for durability.

Library of Congress Cataloging-in-Publication Data

Names: Robertson, Kristin, 1975- author.
Title: Chance of lightning / Kristin Robertson.
Description: Denton, TX : University of North Texas, 2025. | Series: Vassar
     Miller Prize in Poetry ; 32
Identifiers: LCCN 2025003886 (print) | LCCN 2025003887 (ebook) |
     ISBN 9781574419672 (paperback) | ISBN 9781574419757 (ebook)
Subjects: LCGFT: Poetry.
Classification: LCC PS3618.O316975 C47 2025 (print) | LCC PS3618.O316975
     (ebook) | DDC 811/.6--dc23/eng/20250221
LC record available at https://lccn.loc.gov/2025003886
LC ebook record available at https://lccn.loc.gov/2025003887

Chance of Lightning is Number 32 in the Vassar Miller Prize in Poetry Series

Cover image: Jason M. Saunders, *Tear Drop*, lottery tickets on wood sealed in epoxy resin

The electronic edition of this book was made possible by the support of the Vick Family Foundation.

for Sean
and for Heron, like the bird

CONTENTS

IN LIEU OF

Our matriarch says we're not a cemetery-
visiting family, but she knows who is:
the next of kin who sent the telephone
fashioned entirely of flowers with the banner

Jesus Called, Vera Answered. Tonight, no wake,
no funeral procession. Instead, we crack glow
bracelets on the beach. Float seaweed bouquets
knotted with washed-up bits of fishing line.

We hold open a Winn-Dixie sack of ashes.
All seven of us dip a wet finger into the bag
to the first joint, stick it into our mouth
(upend the rest perfunctorily into thigh-deep surf),

and swallow her to hum inside us like a dead
ringer for a trapped moth or backup generator.

WATER STRIDERS

The psychiatrist tells her
to treat her life like
a science experiment.
And later the maze
through the biology building
to take a class begins
with signs masking-taped
to double doors:
Do not let out water striders.
In the bathroom she finds Jesus
bugs wandered away
from the graduate lab
and walking on water
in a stopped-up sink.
That night in her basement
in ankle-deep rain
she will light a pilot light
under the skitter of live wires.
Over her head sparks will fall
like flares. And in a month
before choosing not
to evacuate before a hurricane,
she'll write her social
security number on her arm
with waterproof eyeliner
like a label on a test tube.
But now with a doorstop
and a pencil, she pries open
the bathroom window
to tempt the pond skaters
with a body of water, some

sharkpool for the brokenhearted.
When she calls them graceful,
and when she calls them
merciful, what she really means
is science. Of course they just
hover there in front of her
like goddamned miracles
as if hitting their antennae
against imaginary glass.

LOTTERY

A chance so close to zero, zero's a baby
pool shoved against your screen door

thirty-six thousand feet below this airplane
where a preschooler chokes on a pretzel.

The passengers stand and clutch their necks
as the mother scrapes her finger down

the girl's throat. *You're living in despair,*
the psychiatrist said back home. Long after

she forgets she once stopped breathing,
the girl asks if the plane ever falls from the sky.

Sometimes it does, you say. *Sometimes it does.*
One in eleven million. And when she says,

They'll catch us, the yellow trees, you see
the start of a ginkgo tunnel: You haven't lost

a baby. You go to work, sell tires, rinse
your feet at dusk in your makeshift plastic

pond, where soon all the suns will float:
The bright petals you won't win, but find.

LOTTERY

One man bought a gazebo and some screen
and white doves numbering in the dozens.

He started a dove-release business. Of course
he didn't charge, he did it all for free,

and when he walked up with his cages,
wedding guests, their hands at first to their

mouths, and then down and open in wait
to receive what he had for them, a trembling

life, that gesture was such the offering, blowing
kisses toward him. And what loneliness

couldn't be put asunder when in the night
they flew back always, always to him.

LIFT THE MORATORIUM
ON ANGELS

in this poem one sec for Pearl Vision
and an optometrist who looks exactly
like an uncle who died two years ago.
He's saying *quick puff of air* and *hot air*
balloon in the distance   look through
here   see it   see it now?   and now?
But this, this is the good part: He asks
out of the blue, out of thin, thin air—
Do you still read books? You've never
laid eyes on this man before. You just
moved here. Still like pond water. Like—
wait—lift the moratorium on deer too,
one brief moment—still like the ears
of the mother and her fawn behind
the privacy fence. It's only been two
years. Of course you read books. Still.
How much time has passed in his nebula
of wings? You say yes. *Yes, I read.* And
get this: He smiles. He smiles and nods
and adjusts the lenses in the phoropter.
Since your lease is one year and you
won't return for your follow-up, you ask
if he's happy, if where he is now is
better. He chuckles but stays behind
the machine: *Tell me which one is less*
blurry. A or B. A or B.   Here.   Or here.

MAN WAKES UP IN MORGUE AFTER BEING DECLARED DEAD BY THREE SEPARATE DOCTORS

—with a title from I Fucking Love Science

A few of us walk on the moon. Into the night,
many more dip white grapes into glitter

for science fair Andromedas. I papier-mâchéd
star systems and stared at my wife until I died.

Or didn't. To me, what she was was all this planet
could fiddlehead or feldspar or flight path.

I told the mortician and then the paramedic
I had no last-thing-I-could-remember, but the truth is

we end up in wonder. At midnight my wife fed
the contents of our refrigerator to a herd

of about sixty deer, cold and desperate, before I fell
asleep and woke up here. In my last memory,

my wife offers from her hands our spiral
galaxies. The deer hold open their mouths.

GRAVEDIGGER

The night after surgery, our father sends
a photo of the stump, a root-bound plant,
eased from its pot. Like an orphanage nun
I want to swaddle his amputated leg
and hand over the bundle to whoever holds
a train ticket from this war-torn city.
Years ago, after they first married,
he ran naked, dripping from the hot tub,
through their backyard and lit tiki torches
for my stepmother. He conjured wildfires,
his footprints in snow like the reindeer
he was. As a teenager, he dug graves.
Young and strong, my mother says,
he had nothing better to do with his time.
You know how they say hiking is just
walking? Graves are just holes. Except
there are coffin templates, a science
to the shoring of the edges, a science
to the depth and weight. Weekends with
Dad we wandered the town's one museum,
glass boxes of wool coats, pinned-up pants.
Surgeons cantilevered bullets into mouths
of their patients, men set to lose a limb
or two. By our third or fourth visit,
we lined up the bite marks to our teeth.
Then we'd go to what our father called
a bird sanctuary. Sitting in the field
after drive-thru burgers, we never saw
a single bird. I know now a graveyard
is just grass. Unchained clover. Before
the spades and tarpaulins, it's hard earth,
orchestras of crickets, and in your arms
whatever you've carried there to bury.

THE ONLY SOCIAL PART
OF THE SQUID

is the indigestible triangular beak in a kaleidoscope
with other beaks in the belly of a sperm whale.

Squid just prefer solitude. But here we are, wearing
squid headpieces, long iridescent tentacles down

to our jeans, the two of us a rare squid family.
My daughter hops over to un-cephalopod-ed girls

for hide and seek, and I strike up with their mother:
The gorgeous new jellyfish exhibit! It's like graceful

entrails in slow motion. It's sunset hair. She says she
isn't their mother. Their mom, her sister-in-law, recently

killed herself. So she's filled the days with museums
and movies and the aquarium with its half million

gallons of water. One girl lies under a bench, still
as a stingray save her chest rising and falling.

The movers are packing up her house. The woman hides
a tissue in her fist. Her other niece sneaks behind

a larger-than-life cardboard reef shark, but my squid isn't
with her. The exhibits have closed, so I duck under

velvet ropes and wander down ramps. Once I'm under-
water, I speak to a darkness I know all too well:

They're beautiful. Somewhere my only child twirls
with tentacles like handlebar streamers. I know the mother

is here watching her wide-eyed girls, their fingers
and breath against foot-thick glass. Any ghost would be.

LEXICAL CLONING

On his first day, the resident calls
his mother to say he's a *doctor* doctor.

She answers, Yes yes! to confirm his *doctor*
and her *yes*. She tells him his *doctor* doctor

is lexical cloning, repeating a word to indicate
the prototypical meaning is intended,

but hers is something else: epizeuxis,
repeating a word for emphasis. Ten hours

later, when he's offered for dinner the other
half of a granola bar, he says he wants

food food. And even later, almost midnight,
he asks a crying woman to follow him

into the small room, and he says, Did not
survive. And then she asks, *Dead* dead?

He remembers medical school, his first day,
when he still dreamed about entomology.

So the woman in shock will understand
her husband is gone, he reaches for her hand

and says, Dead dead. Once the word *epizeuxis*
to him meant only a species of silver moth.

LOTTERY

I'll build a house with a dozen skylights,
give each a vacancy sign spinning
like a weathervane. Buy cars with oversized
windshields. Skip rocks so cracks flatline
across their fields of vision. This is how
the dead get in. I'll clear acres of land,
a controlled burn, just for the mist,
a ghost's most hospitable environment.

And all the money in the world will,
in fact, bring you back. With the loves
of the lives, even the heat-stroked
carriage horses, the finless sharks,
I'll wait for your number to be called.
Neon rain on the skylights like applause.

MEET THE OWL WITH EYES
LIKE THE NIGHT SKY

—with a title from I Fucking Love Science

She knew the boy who plucked out his glass eye
on the bus to distract the match-lighting boys,

the bigger boys, from setting his only jacket on fire.
She played Marco Polo with him in the community pool,

and every drowned pebble, every concrete chip
sent her hopping to the edge screaming *the eye*

the eye   the eye. And then one day in English class
he skipped a rock between the desks during *King Lear.*

Only it wasn't a rock. It was his glass eye,
and they tossed it to each other with a stage whisper—

Out, vile jelly!—until the teacher cleared her throat,
and to save him she hid it under her tongue

for the rest of that year and the next and the next.
And it felt like a love story in her mouth,

as brilliant as a planet, a piece of galaxy aflame
in the distance, always watching her wherever she swam.

LOTTERY

Vera at the DMV bought a ticket after being struck by lightning. Not the Vera at window A8, Vera at A7. She'd stood alone on the golf course holding a metal pole, and a tall woman anyway. That same day, a shark attacked her. She wore yellow, after all. Swam at night covered in blood. She brushed the storm grate of its gills, thrashed and screamed, just as she had with the mountain lion and the asteroid. In her kitchen Vera A7 fed her prize-winning peppers to a deadly hippo as it cracked the ceramic tiles and pondered dragging her back to its stream. One chance in two million. On her flight to collect her winnings, the dead-stick plane falling quiet as the plague, she knew she'd never be a saint, nine million to one. But on the way down she did end up an astronaut. Through the window, her elbow somehow grazed an icy ring, and Vera knew to whisper *Saturn* to the empty seats beside her, the farthest reaches of her loneliness. Saturn, the god of the harvest, every varietal of squash: the delicata, the crookneck, the ambercup, the carnival, and the fairytale.

LOTTERY

She decides to cut life-size octopuses
out of paper—the Japanese art of Kirie—

instead of flying to Alpha Centauri,
so she spends her winnings on reams

delivered by drivers she invites inside
and asks to model her cephalopods.

They take months to bring to life even if
she slices and slivers most night hours.

She says: *Try this.* Over their hands,
the delicate swirls like aquatic lace.

The men stand in her foyer like statues
afraid to tear, to awaken the tentacles

draped about their wrists and elbows.
And days she feels sadder than dammit

she serves them seawater from a tea set
and counts her single sheets of paper.

Since the deliverymen have brought
her thousands, they wait forever—

her veils of suckers. Once or twice she
cuts them a maze. Octopuses are smart.

One driver asks if there is a word for
the three of them, like a swarm or pod

or quiver. She lifts her X-Acto from her
paper ink sack: *An octopus lives alone.*

No collective noun. He says, *I only know
a group of chameleons is called a starship.*

CASSOWARY

I never planned to track down
every person I ever kissed, but
after I win the lottery and stumble
into Collier, my junior prom date,
on the metro in Madrid, it becomes
my thing. I even gather souvenirs.
From Collier a paper fan, Picasso's
Guernica accordioned inside it:
the bull, the flames, the women
screaming. Collier's friend
Leland (may he rest) sleepwalked
upstairs during a housefire, so
I drive to the field where
we traded spit only once.
I liked breathing his name
Leland in the baseball diamond,
my hands field-chalked into
snowy owls, so I funnel
the marking powder into a vial
of coke on Becca's keychain.
Becca also a one-off, a make-
shift porch party, my boyfriend
busy under some overpass
spray-painting *Nightwatchman*.
When I find him in Cabbagetown,
he apologizes for the abortions,

both of them, twenty years like
yesterday, asks to bum money
for Newports. I unfold what
I have on me into green wings.
When he fumbles his lighter,
I slip it into my jeans, the fifth
pocket, otherwise useless.
They weren't all like this.
Some I loved: Jamie Webb
in third grade who died looking up.
In a lightning storm, he gripped
the tent pole. His mother writes
coordinates along the tendons
of my wrist. When I follow them
to an outlet mall, I cry and buy
a pretzel. I wash my ventral
tendon like a ventral fin,
and I do swim out to an offshore
oil rig where I reunite with
the heroin dealer I loved for
six years. Mike offers a tar ball,
names the shells I collected
on my swim Grace and Grace
and Grace, just like his cats.
Brian was allergic, but he slept
on the floor of my hospital room
for ten nights and married me.
He had nothing else to give
beyond divorce papers and
seventeen crystal flutes I smashed
for glitter the Halloween I ended up
at the Clermont Lounge and fell
in love for an hour with a stripper.
Chandra worked the unlit end

of a match into her nipple.
Between songs, she explained
Chandra means moon in Sanskrit,
as in *chandrasana*, half the moon.
We meet for tea. She doesn't remember
me, of course, but she pretends.
I slide an envelope of my windfall
up the stripper's thigh, and Chandra
says *Don't go turning what I give you*
as a souvenir into a bird. Only it is
a bird, a stolen cassowary from
the Atlanta Zoo. I walk it twelve
blocks to the subway, cradle its
oceanic neck and vestigial spike
in my lap, along with the lit match,
the glitter, the Graces. The latitudes
and lightning, the owl vials and
housefires, the bulls and screams.
All the diamonds. *It might be used*
to attract a mate, he says, the man
next to me, as he traces the cassowary's
crest. *But no one knows for sure.*
From his small backpack, the bird's
favorite: a fallen plum eaten whole.

PORTRAIT OF LOVE AS FAILED VOCABULARY QUIZ

May I call you endeavor? May I call you
gingerly? I haven your sleek and luminous
ovation. My ardent of the mercenary, I'll infinite
the wrangle, hovering and turbulent, for you.
Sublime citadel, listen to this intricate as it
teems. Let's muse your decipher like a serene,
a voracious. Let's just connoisseur. Is this
an awry between us or a crusade? Say era.
Say epoch. I gather handfuls of the panoramas
and the culminate: Say yes. I will comb your
legendary, straighten your desolate. My mouth
staminas ever ever for your succumb. Don't you
hear the fluster, that sweet forfeit? You still
phenomenon me. Together, we phenomena.

WIND CHIME

When you aren't home by one
You'd said ten and no call

I grip the edge of our couch
And remember Switzerland

Somewhere high up the side
Of a mountain as if someone

Said *wait here* and just like that
It balanced next to a red church

A goat with its red collar
The clang of its pasture bell

LOTTERY

I bought the word *antediluvian* and filled
my Honda with pairs of strange birds

I bought back from extinction. After
you left, I bought two passenger pigeons

for my passenger seat and two Lord God
birds before they boarded up the bird stores

and spray-painted closed for hurricane.
I'm selling it for parts: *ante-   -diluvian.*

Choose (1) the before or (2) the deluge.
Baby, do you want a pigeon or a passenger?

I don't need cash, so they're a steal. Within
the hour they're reversing interstate lanes.

Take the bird or the God or the Lord. For you
I bought the name it asks to go by and this storm.

PORTRAIT OF LOVE
WITH PALINDROMES

When we met, you called me Hannah.
Or Anna. The lake that morning calm.

So level, your kayak. *Do geese see god?*
you asked as you passed my small boat.

Tattarrattat went my heart. I begged you,
Don't nod—   Ah! Wow.   Wow.

My gorgeous reviver, gorgeous racecar.
This noon, madam, you said. *Air an aria.*

I did anything to know you backward
and forward. Never odd or even. Before you,

my world was no lemon, no melon—just
evil olive with star rats and stack cats.

Was it a rat I saw? Was it a cat I saw?
O, stone, be not so. Amen, icy cinema.

BOTTLE TREE

My tree bloomed its first bottle
the night the guy I used to love

abandoned a dead dog.
The South is crazy with these

trees. Supposed to keep away lost spirits.
He owned a pet crematorium,

and when he couldn't pay the electric bill,
he drove his work truck laden

with lawn bags outside town, stopped
every hundred yards. With each cut

of the engine he jerry-rigged
a kind of lamentation—earth

to earth—and as he lifted the bodies,
a laying on of hands.

By the night of my ex's arrest,
my tree chimed with over a hundred.

What's a compendium of bottles?
A wonderment? A confusion?

I imagine the last cabernet glinted for
a lab-pit mix named Hosanna. In the highest

branch, the wind ceased
at last, and all at once, to howl.

LOTTERY

All y'all should have a stripper song, the song
you would strip to if given the chance, the same

way you should know what you'd do with the money
if you won the largest jackpot ever. Of course

you save the world, the bears and babies, the wrong-
fully convicted and homeless. You go bankrupt

as most winners do. You give the millions away. But
before you do that, drive your brother over

to the Corvette dealership on Lee Highway where folks
in Chattanooga go if they win the largest jackpot ever.

Say to him *Pick two* and mean it. And then you're
ten and eleven again and bottle-rocket happy.

Last June you marched your uncle's ashes down
the shoreline while you twirled black umbrellas

to an imaginary trumpet. Pay cash for that stretch
of Gulf of Mexico beach. In the borrowed Corvette,

a convertible Stingray, crank up "You Shook Me
All Night Long" and pull your tank top over your head.

Fill your backseat with the good macarons, Sphinx
cats, and Ziplocs packed with terrorless diamonds.

DRUG DEALER: A 90S WHIP REEL

Honda Civic DX, Camellia Red. Not red, fuchsia. The color of hives or psoriasis. Thirteen-inch hammers. Baby rims. One snap of my first ride: Girl with pigtail braids, college T-shirt, whiskered jeans. Squinting into the sun, hand to my brow as if headed to the Gold Rush. *Don't go to jail*, my mother says before I turn the key. *Don't go to jail.*

Nissan 240SX, Platinum Ice Metallic. Limousine tint, five-star seventeens. Dorm breezeway drive-by, twelve-inch subs thump my chest, every girl's chest on the campus west side, like a defibrillator. He's the brother of another RA. At his place the cat gives birth on the linoleum floor. He cleans each kitten with a washcloth and names them all Grace. He says, *Don't take your body away*, in the trailer behind his mother's house. *Don't take your body away.*

Mitsubishi 3000GT, Passion Red. To come to a stop, the rear spoiler lifts like a jet flap. In a Rafferty's booth, he writes sixteen and three zeros and a dollar sign on a cocktail napkin and slides it toward me as if I'm his quarterback and this— each X is a kilo—is my clutch play. On the way back to my apartment, corner of a rough street, some kid yells, *Let me hold something.* That night, he reaches behind his back and lays a silver handgun on my biology textbook. He nods to it and says, *That's a Ruger 1911.*

Ferrari F355 Spider, Rosso Corsa. Racing red. I pose in my urban camouflage minidress at the dealership. Last-minute, twelve-hour trip to Miami. I stand up my mom and Joseph and his Amazing Technicolor Dreamcoat. When he claims he lost his cash, I max my two credit cards and book a room at the Best Western. I step foot on South Beach, untie my bikini top, and hand him my camera. On the way home, while he sleeps reclined in the passenger seat, a cop pulls me over for driving alone in the HOV lane.

Honda Prelude SH, White Diamond Pearl. Leased brand new. Backed in to the first spot at the Kinko's where I run copiers overnight to pay for it. I haven't seen him in a while. He asks if he can drive it; he'll bring it right back. I find my car the next day, empty Hennessy bottles under the seats. All morning with him on my futon, and then I work a ten-hour shift. At midnight I drive by his house. Jennifer's Toyota Camry LE V6 in his driveway. Light Blue Metallic, like sky. Like the clouds parting. He stands in his front yard with a gun and threatens to shoot me.

PORTRAIT OF LOVE AS AIRBAG

Heavy geode a Smithsonian docent somehow
offers me, and I cradle it while around me
classmates radiate, use words like
brilliantest and *sparklinger*—

Or the heirloom tomato at the market, against
my hand the heat, layered with Augusts,
and the person for whom I will fall walks up,
takes my wrist, and says *I grew that*—

Or the sea turtle I save more than once,
drop off the boat slip with a *swim come on
swim* and a kiss to the carapace, and my fingers,
out from under its flippers, briny and unladen—

To you, this, this, this
is my head.

PORTRAIT OF LOVE
AS PERIODIC TABLE

I

Hydrogen	You are a rocket around the sun,
Helium	A field day of message-filled balloons,
Lithium	And the power to my Walkman.
Beryllium	This love once as green as emeralds
Boron	Now strong as a twenty-mule team
Carbon	And hard as diamonds. Alive
Nitrogen	As muscle, as protein, as the air
Oxygen	In my lungs. What water, what fire—
Fluorine	I'll show you! Open your mouth
Neon	For *Hot Doughnuts Now.* Open
Sodium	Your heart, salty and reactive, to
Magnesium	Me, the chlorophyll to your leaves,
Aluminum	The foil to your loneliness. Can
Silicon	You lie here in the soil, the sand?

II

	You lie here in the soil, the sand
Phosphorus	And strike matches until we gleam
Sulfur	Like volcanos, run hot as springs.
Chlorine	Remember that night in the pool
Argon	Diving down toward the light,
Potassium	Feeding each other cold french fries,
Calcium	Your teeth like shells, like milk?
Scandium	Wet, we biked to the top of that hill
Titanium	To watch spacecraft, the sapphire
Vanadium	Sky, and then the violet sapphire
Chromium	Of morning. I wanted your steel,
Manganese	Your structures. Dreamed our alloy.
Iron	And today you stand here, this bridge
Cobalt	In the distance, this water so blue.

III

	In the distance, this water so blue,
Nickel	Worth all the money in the world,
Copper	These endless handfuls of coins. Take
Zinc	Them. Take me like a supplement.
Gallium	I will melt in your hands, and we'll
Germanium	See if I can cure whatever ails you.
Arsenic	Yes, I'm poisonous sure, sure, but
Selenium	Good for you. As seeds. As fish.
Bromine	Inside this darkroom, we developed,
Krypton	Became one silhouette in headlights.
Rubidium	If you're lost, I'll be your coordinates.
Strontium	My body, your flare, your firework.
Yttrium	This love: A spark. Hereafter: A lantern.
Zirconium	I said my promises weren't fake.

IV

	I said my promises weren't fake
Niobium	On the fast-train platform in Japan,
Molybdenum	So you set down your missiles. Between
Technetium	Us grew the lightest, human-made star.
Ruthenium	We flipped the switch, sent a current
Rhodium	To searchlights, a mating dance over
Palladium	Dealerships, above plumes of exhaust.
Silver	We managed to shimmer and shimmer
Cadmium	Through copper beech trees, yellow, red.
Indium	Beyond this bright cockpit display,
Tin	Our simple life: Cans of black olives,
Antimony	Flame-retardant toddler pajamas,
Tellurium	Coolers of organic Capri-Suns. You
Iodine	Heal my wounds, filter my water, you.

V

	Heal my wounds, filter my water, you
Xenon	Sexiest of strobes and lighthouses.
Cesium	How much time will it take for you
Barium	To know all of me, inside and out?
Lanthanum	How far can I fly and you still watch?
Cerium	I've watched you. You carry a Zippo
Praseodymium	And don't smoke. You stand to light
Neodymium	A stranger's cigarette. At night you
Promethium	Never speed, your odometer the moon.
Samarium	I'm still drawn to you like a magnet,
Europium	Our life is a couch in technicolor flush.
Gadolinium	When I first got sick, all those scans,
Terbium	You held my hand in fluorescence,
Dysprosium	Held your breath during the MRIs.

VI

	Held your breath during the MRIs
Holmium	And surgeries, my body a laser show,
Erbium	You always wore rose-colored glasses
Thulium	Surrounded by endless x-ray films.
Ytterbium	You see through me, always have.
Lutetium	You learned photodynamic therapies,
Hafnium	Sang *we all live in a yellow submarine*
Tantalum	Next to scary surgical instruments.
Tungsten	You're stronger than anyone I know,
Rhenium	Any coil or filament or rocket engine.
Osmium	You conquered your fear of needles,
Iridium	Of signing powers of attorney and living
Platinum	Wills. You bought us wedding rings
Gold	And a bracelet for a four-year-old.

VII

	A bracelet for a four-year-old
Mercury	Who lets only you take her temperature
Thallium	In the coldest, wintery midnights. Look,
Lead	It's heavy, all of this, the weight, yet
Bismuth	You stayed inside our rainbow fortress.
Polonium	The static electricity that's between us
Astatine	Rare as the most dangerous medicines.
Radon	Our love is in groundwater, in mines,
Francium	Measurable when trapped or cooled,
Radium	Ill-fated as girls with their luminous paint.
Actinium	Incandescent inside the bodies of mice,
Thorium	we glow. Scientists will handle us only
Protactinium	ever with gloves. I'm this green planet.
	You are a rocket around the sun.

PORTRAIT OF LOVE AS CAROUSEL

Fairground organ, barnacled with cherubs,
    all kiddie baroque, and I'm going

nowhere, gasping. Marionetted up and
    down in a canon of show ponies.

Most worth-its in life are cyclical: Lunar phases.
    Wurlitzer beats. At every seventh

second, the blur of a single evergreen.
    Circadian rhythm. In Sierra Diablo,

the Clock of the Long Now. My horse,
    a hundred years old, refurbished, gentle

enough to flash me its teeth. Gums and bridle
    pink and bejeweled, it gallops *Sobre*

las Olas. Wind in my face, eyes blown closed.
    I grip tighter, tighter the gold rope.

NIGHTLIGHTS

You ask why wait until dark
like a couple of crepuscular bats

to find them homes, and I hardly
believe you're still with me,

a woman who misreads *Is it?*
when it says *It is.* In our hallway

of sunset, I'll be damned if you're not
standing there, ready to plug in stars.

LOTTERY

We name our island Aubaine, the native word
for *windfall*, derived from the word for *foreigner*,
and let's face it: We are strangers here. Most dinners
we ate hot dogs off the concrete at the YMCA pool.

We buy every two-hundred-gallon aquarium
we can find and free all the supermarket lobsters.
Lobsters feel anxiety, we tell the reporters, as we unfold
our beach chairs underneath one of our twenty-eight new

wind turbines. How the blades churn like ocean waves.
We can't save everyone, but we can power up
someone's hot plate. Before you toss a crustacean

into the sea, you cut the bands to free its claws.
Toward you, waiting at the end of our pier,
I marionette furious lobster after furious lobster.

PORTRAIT OF LOVE
AS COFFIN NAIL

First sex in months, he whispers *Cold?*
and over his shoulder I answer *blackberry*
winter in two exhales. He asks *What's that?*
Whole weight of his head now on my chest.
After a decade this man from Alaska
where moose tower over Subaru Outbacks
still flinches when I slip in a southernism
as if when on top I might tie an asfidity bag
around his neck, my mother's mother
a gris gris woman from New Orleans.
I think everyone traps spirits in bottle trees
or porch mirrors. Once he did ask what I had
in my pocket, and he still married me that day,
had a baby with me the following Tuesday.
Here it is May again and cold enough to kill
a hog for the boucherie or to feel up a witch.

TO THE COPS WHO
SEARCHED MY HOUSE

When the on-call doctor calls 9-1-1
    and reports a baby at risk, I know

you have to lights-and-sirens to my address,
    face me in my T-shirt and pajama pants,

and ask, Where's your baby? And when I point
    to my belly, I know you still have to

check, even in the washing machine, a hiding
    place I hope has never turned up

a missing anyone. I can tell you guys spike
    beach volleyballs on weekends, crash

in girls' apartments when you're too loaded
    even to walk home along the esplanade.

I bet the two of you mostly use condoms,
    even in your trucks parked just beyond

the piers with their rainbows of light strings.
    I explain I've never met this doctor

who must have misunderstood when I tried
    to tell her I might not have the baby.

There, in my living room, both of you, all
    suntanned and sidearmed, somehow say

easily—*Ma'am, that's not the same   No, it's not
    Not at all*—back and forth to each other

as if passing a box of something, maybe
    seawater, without spilling a single drop.

POEM FOR MY
UNBORN DAUGHTER

Months now I've handed you over
in my dreams. To the tall, strange man

on the subway platform. To nuns.
To the firefighter backing down

the ladder. To the masked surgeon.
The strongest swimmer. From evildoers

I've hidden you on the top shelf
inside a lidless piece of crockery.

My wherewithal to stash you places
never runs out. You fit inside the air

duct at the Cascade Inn, which shares
with Food City a parking lot taped off

for the bald eagle, her nest a crown
of thorns for the Aisle 6 streetlamp.

I've weighted down a duffel bag with
your anchor body, your anvil body.

Instinct, it is, above all else, to save.
When a lab rat's given a choice to eat

chocolate or free another trapped rat,
a stranger it's never seen before, it will,

every time, again and again, lift the door.
I've sewn you pinch by pinch into

my suitcase like a kilo of cocaine.
Mixed you into suet for grackles to smear

onto their asphalt-rainbow wings. Away
from me I've winnowed you like grain.

Tonight I whisper to you, *Please drink*,
as I flag down a river-bound springbok.

BUTTERFLY KOI

swims alone at an off-season beach house
with an empty electronic food dispenser.
Waterline so low the lotus roots wave back.
The koi keeps scaring itself with its own fins,
sweeping the bottom of the shrinking pond.
I imagine it feels like a new angel, all gauze
and yaw. And when it leaps into the air
the first time, we both tread for a moment
in wonder, two Os of mouth, gasping.
Better here than where we've been lately.
The psychiatrist at home put a name to it.
Called it despair. *You're inside despair,*
she said. The second time the koi springs
from the water, a blue heron lands a stone's
throw. How long since it stole the others?
When the whole siege of herons ambles up,
I search for a bucket. The best I can do is
the fish hammocked in my shirt. I read
koi names carved into a post, cradle against me
the abandoned fish. We're surrounded by
gorgeous birds only Dragon has seen up close.

LOTTERY

The middle school fills a quarry on the edge of its land the day
I sub for the English teacher who taught *A Modest Proposal*
the week before and while forty-two weeks pregnant yelled *Eat
the children!* in the hallway. The students love her, of course.
She says *shit* sometimes and *damn it all to hell* when they don't
read. Today they have read the story, even if they don't have
their books after rushing from the ballfield dedication. The
principal handed each student a rock from the historic quarry.
They drop their souvenirs on top of their desks like retrieved
gamebirds. Sit sweaty and breathless. The girls pick their shirts
from their breasts and gather their hair in their fists. The boys
smooth their pants down their thighs. My baby would've been
about this age, this awkward. When the nurse asked if I wanted
to see, I turned toward the monitor, spotted that beautiful oval
hewn into a phosphene. But he isn't mine, the boy who juggles
three rocks from his friends' desks. Or she isn't. The girl who
palms her token stone in the last row. Her ponytail between
her teeth like a bit.

LOTTERY

He buys a tractor, sap green
and bright as a poisonous frog,

and mows football fields
behind local schools,

eats his lunch on bleachers,
pimentos out of the jar.

Never a jazz cat or catcaller,
he claps for the pep girls,

the majorettes, their batons
like deadfall. Before he won,

he lived for chainsaws.
Woodchips like atmosphere,

ticker tape or snow. Now
he buys ticker tape and snow

at the ticker tape store,
at the snow store. Still

he breathes in the rows
he's cut, the thirty yard lines.

Gas-soaked grass acrid
as the armpit of the frog,

the frog alive and wondrous
and full of poison and alone.

COME CORRECT WITH THE ELEGY

for the girlfriend who dates the guy
for a few years off and on and
off again when he up and dies
in his easy chair, the guy who knew
her dog's name but not her dog's name
when she was ten. She's still his
in-case-of-emergency person, but
no one calls her for three days until
she crosses the mind of his one friend
Paul who says Jasmine, the ex she
never met, will handle the execution
of his estate. Jasmine will toss the cross
stitch the girlfriend labored over
when he lost his job: two stick figures—
one bodiless, the other with a body
in her hand like a stick—and the phrase
I got your back. All of it into a rented
dumpster outside the garage the girl
organized on a rainy Saturday when
he air-guitared a tennis racket, relived
his teenage years, sang some song
about the sky falling in. She had
never heard them, his favorite
albums she hummed and hummed.

RENTED FISH

Behind the hotel concierge, a rush hour of suns.
Would you like to pick? He knuckles the glass.

Goldfish startle like a synapse, neurons in search of
dendrites. He lifts a plastic wine cup from its stack.

There must be five hundred in here. He taps, taps.
Beautiful word—arrhythmia—skip of the heart.

These tormented fish zap, zap together into under-
water sparks. He seines with his cup in a zigzag,

both cuffs already wet, seizes a victim, and with
my room key slides it across the counter, some

newfangled negroni with swim bladder and
brain. *It's for loneliness*, he shrugs. How long

can a fish live with so little air? I lift it as if to toast.
Most don't make it to morning. Travelers drop

bags in their doorways to search goldfish on their
phones, to discover they eat from human hands.

They learn colors and perform tricks for a lifespan
of fifteen years. I complicate matters and name

this drowning carp Rebecca at the bottom of my cup
after Rebecca across the street who climbed through

my window and drove me to the ER twice. From her
front lawn, she gave rides in her hot air balloon.

PORTRAIT OF LOVE
AS ORCHID SHOW

Into an airplane hangar-cum-greenhouse,
you transport your prize orchid, all bruise-y
and ethereal, to this orchid joust.
Thirty thousand other orchidists, each

boasts an ethereal bruise. A young, male
orchidist elbows the hand-thrown moon jar
you clutch, milky and womb-like and pale,
and hums Marilyn Manson: *We're all stars*

now as some bizarre dude's mea culpa.
As if handing over your soul at death,
workers set aside your white aorta,
unspool and rip a ticket in a breath.

Oh, milling diaphanous cymbidiums!
We sing: *There's lots of pretty, pretty ones.*

LOTTERY

With my winnings I buy an underwater town
out near Tellico where the TVA flooded farms.

The residents compared it to an execution. No way
to train a hickory tree to hold its breath. The next mayor

will be a catfish, the workmen said, tipping their hard hats.
Hired to move the cemeteries, they disinterred most

of the graves. I travel to my ghost city to listen for
the ones they left, the trapped sailors, their echoes

like a skipping record. Remember that song "Lady" by
Kenny Rogers? Starting today, if you drive the periphery

of the drowned township, you'll hear my loudspeaker:
You have made me what I am and I am yours.

I stand on a submerged silo, my fingertips breach
the surface, searching like a carp's fleshy mouth.

MULLET TOSS

"Gulf Coast's Greatest Beach Party"

Nightfall and Matt tries to make it back
to the RV, slows up when sand turns
to gravel, and slumps onto the beer cooler
he's been dragging like an adolescent pit bull.

As fishing-line-tethered toy sharks circle
his Panama hat, Uncle Jim says, Yeah, you're
done. The tumor that'll kill him in six
months already glimmers inside his bile duct,

like one in thousands of stars above the ocean
and this handful of men of a certain age,
wandering somewhere between legend-
ary beach party and the parking lot. Hours

ago they paid fifteen bucks to underhand-
pitch dead fish over the state line, Alabama to
Florida, to applause, to the winners' bracket
for a ray-finned trophy. But now, as crowds

scatter and strung-up lightbulbs dim one
by one with each round of a corner, they hear
the whirr of the if-only seawater again, this
intertidal zone, and the guys wade there awhile.

But soon bikini-clad girls breeze in, including
Miss Mullet Toss herself, and the cooler opens
to make one more go of it, Matt on his feet,
and no one is sixty or forty or twenty.

With the end of the light, and then the end
of even that light, no one is drunk or stumbling,
lost or sunburned, beautiful or sick. No one
worries if morning will come. Or in what state.

HOW TO SCATTER ASHES

Pull over, the lot of you, for neon spray paint
    on propped-up scrap wood: Boiled peanuts.

Stop again for silver queen corn. The drive
    to the Gulf puts you off Interstate 65 about

halfway, through blink-and-miss towns, family-
    owned spots like the It Don't Matter restaurant.

Make a game out of holding your breath between
    farmhouses and on the bridge over

Choctawhatchee Bay. Check in to a beach motel.
    Hit Tom Thumb for a small jar of mustard.

After you unpack, wade knee deep into the ocean
    with the heavy bag. Nod at the kid

with the downed kite, streamers whipping his face
    as he marches the tideline. If you have nothing

to say, sing *Oh, when the stars fall from the sky.* Sing *I want
    to be in that number* as the gray water ebbs clear.

Behind you shrimp boats seesaw their fishholds home.

LOTTERY

Quit your job at State Tire. Pay off the girl with
your first and last name in the service department

so she leaves too. Quit twice and buy eight acres
on a street named after famous horses: Lucky Debonair.

Bold Venture. Measure your land to the middle,
to an old, untilled garden. Stand in a strip of what is

moon but replace *moon* with *anglerfish lure*
one morning first thing. When a blue jay feather dead-

falls onto the brow of a crocodile mother who's actually
a deer mother you finally have it: the way it felt

when the radiologist entered the room (he never
enters the room) and rested his hand on your arm,

that whir, the *almost there* and then the *there*.
But not the landing, no, it's the takeoff of the jay feather

like a jet fighter, there and then not, the hand of the doctor
back behind smoky glass, the *what the hell just happened*

head of Lucky You, featherless and fear-struck as
the crocodile with her two lure-lit crocodile fawns.

LOTTERY

Our stunning glitters are made up of a chunky crackle glitter
which catches the light beautiful giving the ultimate sparkle
effect on a sunny day —The Glitter Coffin Company

When I die, somebody will ash me
off the stern of a shrimper

or use my body to grow
a tree, but I still dream

the processional dream:
pallbearers and me, sugared

into a catchpenny casket,
painted *sharkbite* or *sunrust*

like a speedboat in a slow crawl
behind the motorcycles' blue

flash. Sexy self-constellation.
In each of the bespoke colors,

I order my showgirl sarcophagi.
Please kill all your engines.

A GIFT FROM MY DEAD CALIFORNIAN HOUSEMATE, OR ANECDOTE OF THE JAR

I capitulated his ghosts were humming in the attic
after he'd conceded there was no attic.

I cradled his teacup Rottweiler named Magic
and sang her the blackbird songs:

All your life, all your life. Take these broken wings.
And the other one, *Pack up all my care and woe.*

Once he'd surrendered his broom handle,
early-morning knocks on the spirits' floorboards,

I thumbed his crosses and crystals with tenderness,
acknowledged the voices when they instructed him

to leap naked off the pier. I even led the rescue copters
astray in the dead of night. (*Bye, bye, blackbird—*)

All of this after he agreed to bequeath me his jar.
Windowsilled with its sisters full of rainwater

and moth-eaten endearments, the jar he said
sat brim with lush left-alones and ordinary lightning.

Everyone warned me about California and its crazies,
so I'm driving this jar back to Tennessee,

where grandmothers ban housecats from nurseries
and during sun-showers the devil beats his wife.

Like nothing else, this jar, a legacy of my housemate
once he was forever out of hand, the moon in.

LOTTERY

The Hubble costs a billion, and I win only a fraction of that, but it's enough to build the world's largest single-aperture telescope for my college roommate I haven't seen in years. I call his mother who says for his occupation he still writes *astronomer* even though he's been a cook at the Huddle (not Hubble) House on Brainerd Road for going on a decade. He got the job after he dropped out of college and off the face of the earth. I ask if he was in a facility, that beautiful, generic word for crazy as a loon, a March hare. I tell his mother I've completed my share of seventy-two-hour holds, that the root of the word *facility* means *gentleness*. His mom says no, but he lived in a tent city on East Eleventh. I park behind the waffle-shaped building, wait for his shift to end, replay my last memory of the two of us camped under a triangle of dorm sheets: He wants to teach me about earthshine, so I let him. I tongue the verbs *wax* and *wane*. I study literature, wish he'd swallow Yeats's *silver bag*, Plath's *annihilating*. Instead, he clips his toenail, holds it up to the flashlight in my hand, whispers *crescent moon*, before he eats it.

LOTTERY

She hides a severed hand in a classroom
in the elementary school closed for summer.
She's bought a cadaver dog named Pike
and must use human corpses. If Pike unearths

only a scent or a shirt, he's depressed for weeks,
won't search. But now he bolts down a hall
of pipe-cleaner sunrays, his frenzy like a mother
with a missing child, her shins scythed

from burweed and jimson. It's this ferocity
she wants, her cold body found and found,
deep water or underground or miles away. Pike will
never make a good pet, but she can drop the leash,

watch him bring any peace, any piece of her home.
He just needs to find her wrist in the dark.

FIRST AID KIT

For when panic begins to vibrate the backs
of your arms like they're the trees and panic is
whatever vibrates the trees, leafhoppers
or helicopters, the psychiatrist tells you
to fill a small bag with handwritten notecards
promising   *this will end   this will not
kill you   this no one ever   died from*
and you add gum and headphones and a votive.
With masking tape and a Sharpie you write
Dymphna Dymphna, each side of the candle,
and draw your best version of a bouquet of lilies.
From patron saint of the nervous, the mad,
the runaways, you'll ask for intercession:
Let you never again leave your nine-year-old
niece at a concert inside the Georgia Dome
and lie on a park bench, count to the right number
of sirens or power lines just to be able to breathe.
Let her never hold up your cell phone light,
one in the thousands of stars. Let her never
sway alone in the dark. Never notice you're gone.

PORTRAIT OF LOVE
FOR JUROR #14

Finding missing kids . . . drones can assist. —Blue Skies Drones

The yellow lab named Pavlov works for free,
rests his head on Alex, who watched it all
that night, his baby brother gone, year three.
Surveillance film projected on the wall:

a thermal-equipped drone for body heat.
Alex rubs Pavlov's ear between his thumb
and finger, sits crisscross under the seat.
The prosecutor points his stick, chews gum.

The judge has ruled them inadmissible:
the trunk, the shovel, blood and hair. He loved
his apples, teacher said, this nonverbal
five-year-old. The schoolyard is now full of

seeds. Jurors watch Exhibit 3: an oval clear
and bright as any star, the warm head of a deer.

FAIL-SAFE SHORTCUT TO HEALING

After I leave the hospital, I buy a houseplant a day.
I water forty-seven staghorn ferns and devil's

ivy to corkscrew around TV remotes and blind pulls.
My bathtub's a greenhouse for moth orchids. The Ficus

demands the most attention. After I bring it home,
it drops its leaves right into my hands as I crouch

knees to chest against its thin trunk. At night the leaves
skid across the hardwood as loud as skateboards.
Turns out a Ficus tree hates change. If you so much as
shove its pot to a new window, the damned thing will

downpour like spider-rain in Argentina or fish-rain
in Australia. Of course, this leaf-shower's nothing like

the list of craziest things that fell from the sky: the cows
and blood. There's also the list called fail-safe shortcuts

to healing with ziplines, professional cuddlers, house
plants. Like this Ficus, or weeping fig. When stressed

it will strangle its own roots. But since day forty-eight,
or last Tuesday, it hasn't rained a single hermit crab.

LOTTERY

With her favorite couple, Philip and Jack,
entomologist and etymologist, respectively,

she buys every sapling trussed into burlap
and dying in parking lots, drags them

by the hair into the primary school for
fifty kids who turn thirty in the year 2040,

when no bees will sleep curled inside
flowers, worrying each other's feet.

Her jackpot buys one hundred and one.
Each child will get two. They reach up

with both hands. Jack teaches them transitive:
to tend, as in *to caretake* + a direct object.

She plants the leftover tree, a pecan.
Mischance means *undergo* + *a misfortune*,

or *to suffer* + *something unfortunate*.
After thirteen years it goes to seed, the first

drupes like four-chambered hearts, heavy
baubles not yet worn. Somebody somewhere

had to've unzipped a backpack mid-
conversation, and a bag of pecans spilled

and softened somehow and burrowed
into dirt to grow into a wild pecan that soon

enough pollinated that lone tree on the edge
of her eight acres. And so what if what

she wants still, after all this time, is to be
loved? Sitting way out there, porch lace-

wing green, she's indehiscent herself, but
she could almost burst. So damn full of hope.

WE MAY HAVE JUST A YEAR TO PREPARE FOR A SUPERVOLCANIC ERUPTION

—with a title from I Fucking Love Science

List the living things to hold on your lap:
Eye of a blue whale the size of a softball.
Head of the camp leader in the tent who said
your eyes. As many plums as you can
and all at once. The once-blooming cereus
flower. Serious wake of common loons' wings,
cold like endless cat's-eye marbles in both fists.

Not the ocean up to your neck, the ocean
with blue whale hearts the size of cars.
At least not first. Board a plane to his fingers,
your wrists and all at once. Fly to the panic
of never having done any of it in firelight.
After the wildfires the camp leader said,
The only trees now so far off. Take him to

the Joshuas who can't even believe the size
of the sunset. Not the shoreline for whimbrels,
always the earliest leavers. Retrace the life
of your mouth: Berries hot from the tailgate
of a Datsun. Busted lip, berries and metal.
The monkfish from Le Krill, where outside
a street artist painted her *baleine bleue*.

Blue whales nudge their one and only calf
to the surface to breathe. In the tent the salt
and smoke of the camp leader's tongue
the summer before he almost died. Lightning,
and all at once. You have just this one year.
The first wilderness you ate? Honeysuckle,
a drop shiny as the stud in an earring gun.

PORTRAIT OF LOVE AS MAGGOTS

I'm sure the makers of Downy would be pleased to know that their
product makes even mummified human skin soft and fragrant.
—*William Bass,* Death's Acre: Inside the Legendary Forensic
Lab the Body Farm Where the Dead Do Tell Tales

I buy a field of corpses for my mom,
enchanted with body farms and Dr. Bass,
his donors stuffed in trunks of cars, their home
forever knee-high weeds. She's a real-ass
scientist now, docent of decompose,
and in my dream the souls squat in the dirt
beside their former arms and legs. She shows
tenderness with body bags, untwists shirts.
And she's as happy as they are, for once.
If not for us she could've been a star.
Instead in single motherhood she bounced
from school to school, taught kids molecular
levels of the cell. Hurrah, dear mom, sharp
as a whip, delight in wriggles under tarps.

PORTRAIT OF LOVE AS
THE WORD *PENULTIMATE*

Afraid of horses, I trample sea oats,
cordgrass, and whatever violet this is
toward mostly mares grazing the dusk's
halfheart. Like latecomers at an outlet store:
everything must go. Home from work
I used to drive oceanward. Sure, an apartment
above the 7-Eleven, but cresting the hill
still felt loose as a rope swing, that gap before
falling, that gap where grace lives, where
brave. See, I never could pronounce *elegiac*
on the first try. Here wild ponies stamp
the shoreline for kettle corn. Here I sprint
up to them, cup their fetlocks, and *shh-shh*
until I get to *shiv* and before, finally, *shiver*.

LOTTERY

Somewhere a waterbird cuts
the first letter of your name
into the lake surface. If it's Vera.

ACKNOWLEDGMENTS

Thank you to the editors and staffs of the following publications in which these poems first appeared, sometimes in different versions:

32 Poems: "Wind Chime"

The Adroit Journal: "Cassowary"

Air/Light: "Lottery (When I die, somebody will ash me)"

The Antioch Review: "Portrait of Love as the Word *Penultimate*"

The Arkansas International: "Mullet Toss"

BOATT: "We May Have Just a Year to Prepare for a Supervolcanic Eruption"

The Cincinnati Review: "Drug Dealer: A 90s Whip Reel"

Five Points: "Bottle Tree"

The Florida Review "To the Cops Who Searched My House"

Four Way Review: "Lift the Moratorium on Angels"

Gulf Coast: "Portrait of Love as Orchid Show," "Portrait of Love with Palindromes"

Kenyon Review Online: "Lottery (He bought a gazebo and some screen)," "Lottery (She builds a house with a dozen skylights)," "Lottery (Vera at the DMV bought a ticket)"

The Massachusetts Review: "Gravedigger"

The Missouri Review: "Portrait of Love as Airbag"

Nashville Review: "Lexical Cloning"

Nelle: "Lottery (The middle school fills a quarry)," "Portrait of Love as Coffin Nail"

New Ohio Review: "Portrait of Love as Failed Vocabulary Quiz"

Pleiades: "Meet the Owl with Eyes Like the Night Sky"

Ploughshares: "In Lieu Of," "The Only Social Part of the Squid"

Poetry Northwest: "How to Scatter Ashes"

Prairie Schooner: "Gift from the Dead Californian Housemate, or Anecdote of the Jar"

The Raleigh Review: "Poem for My Unborn Daughter"

The Rupture: "Lottery (She buys a tractor, sap-green)"

The Southeast Review: "Lottery (I bought the word *antediluvian*)"

Southern Humanities Review: "Lottery (She wants to cut life-size octopuses)," "Lottery (With my winnings I buy an underwater town)"

The Southern Review: "Lottery (A chance so close to zero, zero's a baby)," "Man Wakes Up in Morgue After Being Declared Dead by Three Separate Doctors"

Tinderbox Poetry Journal: "Butterfly Koi," "First-Aid Kit"

The Threepenny Review: "Water Striders"

Thrush: "Portrait of Love as Carousel"

"To the Cops Who Searched My House" was reprinted in *Poetry Daily*.

"Fail-Safe Shortcut to Healing" was published in *Reckoning: Tennessee Writers on 2020*.

"Man Wakes Up in Morgue After Being Declared Dead by Three Separate Doctors," "Meet the Owl with Eyes Like the Night Sky," and "We May Have Just a Year to Prepare for a Supervolcanic Eruption" borrow titles from the website *I Fucking Love Science*: https://www.iflscience.com/.

Thank you to series editor John Poch and to Amy Maddox, Joe Alderman, Ron Chrisman, and everyone at the University of North Texas Press.

Thank you to Melissa Range.

"Mullet Toss" is for Rachel Morgan, Mike Parker, and Matt Robertson.